A Female In A

Poetry Through

By An ...ord

•

First published in eBook 2020

•

© Amy Telford 2020

•

The right of Amy Telford to be identified as the author of this work has been asserted by her in accordance with the Copyright, Designs and Patents Act 1988.

All rights reserved. No part of this publication may be reproduced, stored in or introduced into a retrieval system, or transmitted, in any form, or by any means (electronic, mechanical, photocopying, recording or otherwise) without the prior written permission of the writer. Any person who does any unauthorised act in relation to this publication may be liable to criminal prosecution and civil claims for damages.

Thank you for respecting the hard work of this author.

<u>Dedication</u>

To the stars in the dark night sky, thank you for showing me the way.

My Favourite Teacher

As I am leaving Bookwell today
many teachers have taught me along the way
but the one that helped me gain success
which one is it can you guess?

Here you are I'll give you some clues
to guess which teacher, I liked the best
she is kind helpful and thoughtful too
and here you are another clue
she taught me to read and write
and helped me with my spelling too

And when I struggled with my maths
I eventually passed my rock hard SATS
this picture is my final clue
and as you can see, she is pretty too

now I have described her as best I can
you should know by now that it is MRS LONGMAN
I know that you will continue to help those who struggled too
Mrs Longman I will miss you

Free

I`m feeling very free
how could this possibly be
from months of hell that I got
now I'm free at last

I`m flying high above the clouds
and feeling very happy
lots of ways to cope
and that's what really helps

I`m sitting in my bedroom
thinking things are good
this is not a con
this is how I feel

The truth is out
I feel so good
everything is fine
and I am positive too

Appointments

How many appointments have I had with you?
so many thoughts I have shared with you
who do you think has helped me so much?
I know who it is you

You have helped me through so much
the amount of times I've let you down
by saying I want to self-harm and die
but look at me now how different I am

A new life I have thanks to you
I know you will probably say that's not true
coz your gonna say it's down to me
but not all of it was down to me

It's been two long years of seeing you
to help me be as happy as I have wished
but I guess you're right
things take time

It feels so weird to have to say goodbye
to someone a friend and a helpful man
I guess this poem is a thanks and goodbye
for everything you have helped me with

So now I am going to say goodbye
and I hope I won't have to see you again
I think I also need to seen great big thanks
all the way
thank you, Craig, for everything
I don't know how I could have coped in the last two years
without you

Feelings

I feel so blank inside all the time
I don't know what to do
the thoughts are just so hard to fight
the urges give me such a fright

The voices in my head are very powerful now
they get so angry and very annoying
I just want them to go away
they whine on at me to die and hurt
so maybe I should go to where I belong
heaven

I put on a smile and hide the true me
I try to be happy and ignore the thoughts
and get on with the life I wished I had
I say to the voices to go away
but they get stronger everyday

Life would be good if I was in heaven
I would be happy no more suffering or sorrow
loved ones I would be with and fun I would have
God would help me and make me feel safe
make me happy jolly and bright

Life is crap it always will be
things will never change I will always be the same
I have a crap past that I cannot escape
so, going to heaven is the best choice for me
and soon I shall succeed and die very soon

Grandad's Garden

Our Grandad kept a garden,

A garden of the heart.

He planted all the good things,

That gave our lives their start.

He turned us to the sunshine

And encouraged us to dream,

Fostering and nurturing the seeds of self-esteem.

And when the winds and rain came,

He protected us enough,

But not too much because he knew,

We would stand up strong and tough.

His constant good example,

Always taught us right from wrong,

Markers for our pathway that will last a lifetime long.

We are our Grandad's garden,

We are his legacy.

Thank you, Grandad,

I used to be happy

I used to be happy
I used to be skinny
I used to be confident
Funny and giddy

But now all I am is a fat lazy gal
Who has scars up her arms
That run deeper than skin

I have permanent pain etched on my face
Always a shadow of the girl that once was
Happy and bubbly carefree and not sad

But now all they see is a small distant smile
Of the person I was and not who I am

<u>Expression</u>

Standing in the playground
standing all alone
there I see the bullies
my heart goes a beat to fast

Sitting in the classroom
then I hear calls
calls that make you wanna cry
and names that don't make sense

Feeling all along now
sometimes I think its better
sitting in my bedroom
thinking I need help

I'm crying really bad now
It's time I told my parents
I walk the dreaded walk down my landing stairs

My parents are so supportive
I don't know what I would do
without them I don't think I would manage
the torment that I faced

sitting in the drs waiting to get help
realizing the severity
of my messed-up life

Talking to a councillor

talking about what's happened
I see I'm getting help now
that's what really counts

Feeling lots more positive
now I face my new school
learning lots of coping mechanisms
I think this will really help

Walking to my new school
I'm so nervous but who is not
seeing lots of happy faces
makes me happy too
people are so friendly here
I don't know how they could be so cruel at my old school

<u>New Beginnings</u>

Standing with my new friends
feeling very happy
managing to socialize
feeling more relaxed

Sitting in my lessons
working very hard
no one is annoying me
that's what really counts

No bullies are in sight here
and everyone's so friendly
there's lots of help
and things to do
and many friends too

Talking to my psychologist
talking about my friends
he sees I'm lots more happy
and is pleased with what he hears

The teachers are so friendly
and understanding too
they really are amazing
and I really think its true

Sue is very helpful
and very thoughtful too
sue listens to my worries
and helps me understand

My family lots more positive
less arguments I hear
we're feeling more relaxed
and very happy too

I really can't believe
how far I've came along
I'm just so very grateful
for all the help I have

I'm feeling lots more positive
of what the next two years will bring
lots of happy memories
and lots more friends to make

<u>Forget</u>

Forget the bullies
forget the worries
the past
the lot and all things bad

My life is better
without those things
its happy joyful
and amazing too

The past doesn't matter
the futures better
the memories will always remain

I can reflect but also not get upset
I bet I can be positive too

My life's so good
without those things
the past doesn't matter
the futures better

<u>Happiness</u>

Happiness is everything
it means the world to me
to see other people happy and feel it for myself

What would the world be?
without happiness
a lonely place
an unhappy place
and lots of sad faces

Happiness is the best
of all the things in life
the memories we have from it
will always be with us

Happiness is everything
it means the world to me
it brings me lots of happy memories
and makes me feel very positive

Happiness brings lots of things
like friends and all things good
it brings me joy and laughter
and also brings me love

<u>Urges</u>

My urges are so hard to fight
they come and go quite often
some of them are very bad
and some are rather minor

Sometimes I see no other way
of expressing how I feel
writing seems the only way
to make me understand it

But then I do rethink my thoughts
and think of all the good things
life is too good to throw away
from a tiny mistake I did make

ICE is also very helpful
feeling cold and numbness
it makes it feel like I have cut
even though I have not
the water dripping from the ice
feels so good in many ways

My urges are so hard to fight
they come and go quite often
maybe one day I won't have these urges
then things won't seem such a splurge

The YPU

The YPU is a place of help
a place you can regain your strength
a place you can feel so safe
even though you may miss home

The YPU is an awesome place
it makes me appreciate the things I've got
it helped me to turn my thoughts around
so that I feel more positive

Things have changed since I've been here
it helped me to get through this very tough time
a happier girl i now feel
and I smiley girl you now see

This unit has helped me on my way
to a positive recovery
although I have found it hard to cope
and ended up doing silly things
I may regret what I have done
but what's the point in dwelling on it

A better person I've become
a happier person you now can see
I'm now on the way to recovery
thanks to the YPU

Blade

This blade is my heaven
it makes me feel so better
cutting I feel is the only way
of disappearing the sorrow that I face

Sitting in my bedroom
holding this worthy blade
thinking of the consequences
that may come my way

Running it across my foot
seeing the blood and feeling the pain
helps a great deal in many ways

Waking up the next day
realizing what I've done
realizing I need to change
and asking for help is what I need

This blade is my heaven
my only place I feel so good
please oh please don't take it away
it's my only source of hope

My life

My life is the worst life
my life is a stupid one
why was I even put on this earth?
coz my life has no meaning

I really do hate myself
I really do its true
what is the point in my life?
no point I guess

Why do I get bullied?
why do I get the blame?
why oh why do I feel this crap
and why I am I being told I don't get bullied
why am I told that I am a bully?

I really am sick to death
of the torments that I'm facing
maybe suicide is the best option
it would end all the pain
the bullies and upset
I'd be able to go to heaven
and be with my good old Gran

Maybe one day I will get that chance
and maybe I will even love the chance
life isn't good its worthless too
even the bullies agree

My Gran

My Gran was the best
the best Gran you could have met
she was caring helpful and thoughtful too
and helped me get through those rock-hard times

Gran used to bake cakes
many flavours and tastes
she loved her cakes
she made them nice
I always used to help her

Gran used to look after me when I was off school
and make me pancakes on pancake day
my Gran always cared for me
and looked after me on the bad days that I had

The memories I have of Gran
will live on in my heart forever
I will never forget you
and I will miss you lots

I've been on a ride

I've been on a ride a very big ride
I learned so much that I shall never forget
this ride has been tough but strength I gained
close friends I've made and memories that will always remain

I've been at the unit for ages now
and I'm feeling better and positive too
who would have thought I would be here today?
saying I'm happy smiley and laughy

The YPU has helped me lots
and I really appreciate the help I got
I guess I'm gonna have to say goodbye
and jump back onto life's rollercoaster ride

It's on I move to a happier me
I know it will be hard but I will succeed
I'm going to do it and do it well
and prove I am now a stronger me
its back to the big world to say hello yet again
and say goodbye to a very big support network I had

Prudhoe

I'm holding Bertie close to me
keeping tight hold of the memories
Prudhoe has helped me on the way
to a positive recovery

Jean was awesome
the bee's knees too
lots of memories
we did share
getting messy and 1:1`s
I miss her lots and lots
the card is all I have of her
but it means a lot to me
the memories will last forever
and its keeping me going strong

Prudhoe WAS the place to be
when the going got very tough
but now the going feels easier
home is the place to be

Prudhoe helped me lots and lots
it made me realize not to die
lots of coping mechanisms I did learn
and now I am coping very well

Lonely house in the woods

Walking through the woods tonight
scary trees do I see
tall ones pointy one old ones
ooooh the woods are very scary

Owls are hooting
midnight dawning
full moon shining down on me

Think I see normality
staring strongly back at me
but what can this be

Frightened

Frightened is the way I feel
most of the time this is true
I don't know how to deal with it
and I end up being paranoid

The bullies have scared me
they've frightened me to death
I can't leave my house alone
one day I want to be ok
and live a normal life like you

I really don't like this feeling
I just want to be healing
from the hatred that has scared me
through the past four years

I really just want to be normal
and live happy and feel safe
for I know this will happen
I hope its sometime soon

If it wasn't for those cowards
I wouldn't feel this scared
for I just want that feeling
of something that is healing

I know right now I'm frightened
and most of the time its true

I end up feeling paranoid
and feeling very scared

Why can't this healing feeling
stay with me all the time
I like that healing feeling
it makes me feel I'm healing

There once was a girl

There once was a girl
she had cuts up her arms
the one on her neck
the most shocking of all

16 stitches ran across her neck
and bandages covered her arms
she held out her arm
and said she needs help

The doctors were sat there
staring at her she tells them the truth
the doctors say her problems are acute
I am detaining you under section 3
but wait doctor you have no right
yes, I have rights
I am an adult she said

On does she go to a unit called Hadrian
worse she does get with each day that goes by
voices in her head go round and round
shouting and screaming just cut just die

She then gets transferred to a PICU in Yorkshire
assessments enduring and finally a friend
she hopes that soon this mental torture will END

You Make Me

You make me laugh
you make me smile
you help me make my dreams come true

You taught me how to ask for help
you taught me hope when feeling low
you've also taught me love and grace
and how to face each single day

You made me cry
you made me mad
you've built me up and knocked me down
I'm almost like a Lego house

I will not hide of be deterred
I'll always show my pretty face
my strength will be forever strong
and love and hope shall live on

An exciting day trip

A stripy dress the wrong-coloured tights
no shoes to wear a manic rush
the pressures on to look the part

An award to give some lines to say
an anxious yet excited mood
a date not quite that far away
supporting staff and colleges too

The car journey was very fun
all of us facing the unbeknown
n energy drink a real kick start
lots of jokes and laughing too

A posh hotel lots of people
how can I do this I'm too scared
Victoria Gayle and Dom
Amy Lleeche Alexa and Faye
all the staff to lean upon
confidence building hour by hour

A lovely three course meal we had
socializing meeting new people
conversations flowing
relaxing atmosphere happy times

Learning of developments and all that we've achieved
I feel proud to be a part of Tracscare as a team

My big moment has arrived I'm on stage with Victoria

to present best newcomer award

adrenaline pumping through my body

we call the finalists to the stage and watched the videos that are
played

presented with the award they stand and take a bow

Our day comes to an end with jokes about bread and best wishes to
all

we achieved so much as a team and individuals too

thank you so much for such a wonderful day

The ship

I was alive
with motors roaring
travelling places far away

Destinations wide horizons
Cuba Spain Venice too
sunny sites and wide blue sea
waves are crashing under me

Bright and shiny did I feel
hustle bustle on my decks
proud to sails the oceans blue
proud to make their dreams come true

Never quite children laughing
clinking glasses captain shouting
engines booming horns are blaring
always moving never sleeping

Years have passed and how I've changed
rust has now come over me
embedded in this silt and sand
still and quiet do I lie

Gentle calling of the gulls
dogs and walkers passing by
whispering murmurs of the wind
round my empty decks
contented feelings happy memories
of sailing days now long gone by

They won't win

Stand up fight be brave
they say words won't harm me
but what about the sticks and stones
they break me only less than words
the piercing voices of bullies live on
taunting and haunting each day of my life
only I hide behind those bars that shadow me
yet they wrote the book of my past
intention on destruction for the rest of my days
the flashback they come thick and fast
like flashes from a press camera
if only they were not
constantly wishing to delete or rip
into tiny pieces that can't be fixed
now that I am strong, they mean nothing to me
knowing their lives are not what they wished them to be
they're long for a life worth living
only I'm building that life that's worth living

Together we fight

Together we fight we fight as one
because together we make a team
we will fight the good fight
be it a fight for life
or to fight a fight
or maybe fight for your human rights
but fight the good fight
try your best you may not succeed
but try again, again and again
then maybe one day you may win the fight
you will succeed if you fight the good fight
you were taught right from wrong
just value your values
you may not be strong
you might just be idle
look at your role model
value your idol
make sure you smile
always be happy because it's the greatest gift
and please just remember fight the good fight

There's a world out there

There's a world out there
in that wide open air
where people stand and stare
at the labels people gave you

You scream and shout and cry
set me free I am fine
but deep down you know you're not
you're begging them to help

It's so obvious your different
you stand out in the crowd
but your labels will not rule you
who are you to kid?

Sitting in the corner
watching people talk
but no eye contact do I give them
I just sit there listening in
Asperger's has its perks
because I feel like a spy

My memory is ridiculous
I remember random things
like where dad put the screwdriver
I did not know he had

Receipt collections fun

it makes my head make sense
it makes me feel so calm
and diminishes my stress

The labels people gave me
they will not rule my life
I will stand up and be strong
and learn new ways to cope

Frinton

The first few months in rip proofs
my wounds are slowly healing
Amanda changing dressings
and ward rounds always weekly

2:1 arms length no cigarettes or air
no hiding under blankets staff on high alert
in my room all day bantering with staff
each day a new beginning
with love and hope and faith

Muffin man impressions
TV a huge reward
our favourite tunes are playing
whilst we sing and dance along

Card games we played many
magazines without the staples
alarms were sounding daily
patients come and go

Ward access was gained slowly
new friendships were unfolding
close friends we now speak daily
progress we now are making

1;1`s with mark serious or funny
he always understood me

learning ways to cope with life
maybe someone is believing

No turning back the time
nor holding in regrets
they only make me guilty
and stop my life abruptly

Now that new chapters are unfolding
I look back and realize
St Andrews Frinton ward saved my life

Crohn's

I sit calmly then make a race

To what has become my throne

I have to postpone

Plans that had once grown

The pain that it gives me is deep

Twisting and cramping is real

Sometimes it is overwhelming

And causes a hospital stay

Its toxic air i cannot hide

A constant reminder

My crohn's is never sleeping

Fatigue its a constant battle

Coffee-is it a risk worth taking?

Planning ahead is always advised

Toilet seeking in disguise

Steroids they make me bloated

Liquid diet i will promote it

It reduces the inflammation

In a positive less risky way

Flares they may happen often

Or maybe far in-between

Just watch for the subtle signs

And catch it before you fall on your knees

From ashes I will rise

From the ashes i will rise

From the deep pits of despair

like a phoenix I will evolve

a new life a new hope

With the fire dampened down

all the pain of yesterday

may be concrete in my soul

but failure past and present

plants the good seed of success

Harvest all the special moments

soak in the light of hope

because even if I stumble

I will surely rise again

Mitford

A place of hope a place for care

a place that understands my needs

a place that helps to exceed

life's impossibilities

Skills I am learning day by day

confidence building month by month

trusting staff and opening up

demons vanishing no power they have

Daily outings they me happy

crafting relaxing in my flat

fun times are had and memories created

illustrated on our faces

MDTs and CPAs show the progress I have made

positive outcomes make me proud

one step closer to recovery

No issue is an issue here

staff have respect and dignity

they'll talk it through and through again

which helps relive anxiety

staff have taught me many things

from crafting skills to living skills

they've taught me how to love myself

and I how I can achieve my goals

Autistic Means I Am Different

Autistic means I am different
The world I see unique
Not your neurotypical norm
Maybe not on form

Emotions are so hard to know
A mixture I may not understand
Leads to meltdowns
I often stim or may need quiet time

Masking is my forte
I have to hide my inner self
Because the things that make me different
Not many understand

Social cues they don't come naturally
I tend to mimic others
I try to fit in to an unrealistic world
But all the time I know I'm different

Sensory overload is painful
I may shut down
White noise is very soothing
Hedgehog balls relieving
Pressure very grounding
But each individual unique

I am proud of who I am
Of how I've learned to cope
Not embarrassed by my ways
I love my little quirks
they make me who I am
I am autistic

Acknowledgements

To my family, thank you for never giving up on me, for fighting for me during my most dark and desperate years, for believing in me when I had no belief in myself, for the endless love and support.

To my late gran and grandad, for your wise words.

To Papworth Hospital, for saving my life when I was on the brink of death.

A special thank you to Sam Burnell and Kirsty Charlton for making this book possible.

To the SHINE charity which supports CNTW This charity helps support CNTW service users and makes a real difference to people's lives. Thank you for providing the funding to help get this book published.

To CNTW and Team Mitford, for allowing me to discover myself and understand my Autism, for giving me the skills to live an amazing life of freedom in the community. Thank you to every single team member, for believing in me and showing me the light to a positive future. For the person-centred care compassion and love, you will all hold a special place in my heart.

To Geoff and everyone at speak up self-advocacy, thank you for introducing me to expert by experience work and for all the support you continue to give me throughout.

To Stephanie, Anna and all my closest friends, for the inspiration and support, for believing in me and encouraging me to achieve what I thought was impossible.

To Orbis Support, for helping me to continue my Journey into the community and achieve my lifelong dreams. For the endless care and compassion, you show not only to myself but to all people within your care. for the dedication and individualized care.

Most importantly to all those who have helped me become the person I am today. For being a part of my journey and keeping my spirits high throughout my most difficult days.

Printed in Great Britain
by Amazon